LISTEN WITH YOUR HEART

I have a very special person in my life. He's my friend, my soul mate, my lover and my husband. We've been together for over fifty-five years. We were together for four years before we got married and this year adds fifty- six more.

Three years ago we moved into the most wonderful place in the world. The apartment complex I was looking at was great but I fell walking out the door and broke my leg. I am already on oxygen so my husband went out and found an apartment for us. This is the place that we are currently at. With the help of my family and five of the seven children, we moved out of the house we've been in for over forty-four years. It's a good thing my memories are great, because they tore the house down.

After getting rid of almost everything we owned, we moved into an apartment building with our three dogs. This was the best move we ever made. There are over one hundred units and everyone knows everybody. After being here for about a month I started writing poetry and it's been such an honor to share it with everyone here. Things will happen and I write a poem about it, most times I write from my memory of the children as they were growing up. About fifty percent are about our seven children and the three dogs we have. Poems about respect and love, kindness and treating other people the way you wish to be treated. The rest are written about the country, patriotism, going to war and where we're going with what's happening now. Writing poems about the anger and hate, and the criticism of our president and the dishonor kneeling instead of standing for our National Anthem. My thoughts are varied and sometimes very silly. Some make people laugh and some make people cry.

But, I am asked often to do a reading here. So happy am I to oblige, as I look at my husband and realize he's beaming with pride as I read. Yes, this is our new home. We love it. It's for fifty-five years of age and older. Believe me there are a lot of older people. Forty percent are aged somewhere between seventy to one hundred and at least five of them are over ninety-three. There are also centurions. We now have a new family just as I had with our children. The big difference is that now we get to do this as adults. We socialize, play cards and Bingo, there's a Friday night Happy Hour and we actually sometimes act just like kids do. Laughing, dancing and singing. I wouldn't change it for the world.

WE ARE ALREADY HOME!

Gretchen Eichhorn
April 15, 2020

TABLE OF CONTENTS

Listen With Your Heart... 1

A Perfect Day...2

When I Grow Up...3

A Wing and A Prayer...4
I'll Try Again Tomorrow...5

What's Next...6
Happy Days...7

Downsizing..8
Our New Home...9
And So We Laughed... 10
Bingo Night...11
Happy Hour...12
Our Director...13
Many Thanks... 14

Aging Well... 15
Birthday Wishes.. 16
Today is my Birthday.. 17
I Need to Get to Fifty.. 18
Flowers are for Love.. 19

God's Plan...20
God Changed the Plan.. 21
Before It's Too Late.. 22

Believe.. 23
Days of Yore... 24
Respect...25
If I Could be A Better Me.. 26
Eternity... 27

Family 28

My Dear Child...29

My Garden..30

Family Retreat...31

A Shopping Day..32

Can't Stay...33

Hand in Hand..34

You Are Amazing..35

All of Me...36

My Love..37

Dogs Vacation..38

The Puppy...39

Trying to Quit..40

Cancel the Wedding..41

Depends..42

Man's Invention..43

Lists..44

Something About Nothing...45

Poetry...46

Troubled Thoughts..47

Senior Benefits...48

Shopping on the Internet..49

Just Another Day..50

Carried Away..51

Babies Are Adorable...52

I'm Getting Older...53

Senior Living...54

Medicare and Me..55

My Mother...56

Mother's Rules..57

Mother...58

The Game...59

Who Is She...60

Grandma's Letter..61

Fifty Years..62

You're Gone...63
My Eulogy..64

Music to My Ears..65
The BGC...66

The 21st Century..67
Lost Pride...68
Going to War..69
Troubled Thoughts..70
What I Need..71
Ecology..72
Money..73

The Sewing Machine...74

Friend...75
My Friend..76
My Friend Kim...77

Cloudy Mind...78
Feeling Blue..79
I Love You Still..80
Deep Thoughts...81
Rotten Thoughts...82
Unfinished Arguments...83
My MRI...84
Just A Phone Call...85

Moving Along..86

Lunch With the Girls..87
Second Lunch With the Girls..88
Third Lunch With the Girls..89

Christmas Decor.. 90
It's Almost Christmas..91
Christmas, All is Forgiven...92
Christmas at Home..93

Hushed in the Dark... 94

Listen With Your Heart

Hear me from the start, but listen with your heart.

I love people and things that no one can know. This is who I am.

Sweet talking, fast walking, dancing in the sun, quick kisses, this is how it's done.

Listen from the start but listen with your heart.

You'll hear my tears and fears my hopes and dreams, and ever after it will seem.

You know me now as I had hoped you would, you hear my words as I knew you could.

Listen with your heart when I hurt inside, or how much I cried about something that moved me.

You listened well, and I could tell you listened with your heart.

It's a special person who hears beneath the spoken word and listens with their heart.

A Perfect Day

There's no such thing as a perfect day, but we've come pretty close. Like the day our youngest got married, we were ecstatic for the bride he chose.

Or maybe the birth of our first grandchild so many years ago. She looked like her mother so tiny and sweet she was perfect from her head to her feet.

Possibly the wedding in the backyard years later, when the rain finally stopped. As the sun came out the music started, and all the champagne was popped.

There was the time we were on vacation and everyone was happy that day, we got to play shuffleboard out on the lawn, since we'd never done it that way.

Memories take me back to more perfect days, I believe there are so many more, but the best are the ones with family and friends, these are what I look for.

A perfect day starts with peace of mind, knowing the family is well. Our country is not in an uproar as far as I can tell.

Each day I thank God for my family, and hope it turns into another perfect day that I get to spend with you.

When I Grow Up

When I was young it was so much fun to think about what I'd be.
When I grew up and on my own, mature and at last to be free.

I would drink what I want, eat what I like, and go where I want to go. If I decided to go out in the middle of the night, no one would tell me no!

I'd get an apartment, entertaining my friends, and we'd party until the wee hours.The routine was nothing more than work and then home, then dinner and a quick shower.

To pay room and board I worked from 9-5, and my pay check was very small. This wasn't living I could barely survive, and I had no social life at all.

The next best thing was get married. Okay! The freedom to come and go as I please. He said, "You won't have to work after all.". Okay I say as I grab my purse and head out to the mall.

Jump ahead six years and five babies later, I'm walking the floor every night, with the baby who cries because she's cutting teeth, and he's snuggled in bed so tight. Four years and three more kids, what was I thinking? I'm washing and cooking and cleaning forever and my hands are always stinking.

The truth is I love my life; the bedlam and joy they all bring. I rush around and stress myself, but I wouldn't change a thing.

Jump ahead ten years we're still in love, my children are now my friends.

Now we have more dogs, and no kids. So when I look around I think I found, my life has just hit the skids.

We move out of our house into an apartment, just like my original plan. But I go nowhere, now a walker is my chair, doing nothing as much as I can.

But he's here with me as I need him to be. as he gently takes my hand; and asks me clear "Would you change anything dear" and I truthfully answer "No."

He kisses me gently holding my hand and it's off to bed we go.

A Wing and a Prayer

I don't enjoy washing, ironing and cleaning as much as I did when I was younger.

Those days are gone; it's new ones I demand. Like company, shopping,
and excitement I hunger.

From age 1-5 I don't remember well; 6-14 weren't great; 15-35 I hit it good.

And by 40 I had too much on my plate.

Starts the decline at oh, 69 that wasn't my best year.

But at 74 I was back out the door and everyone stared to fear.

That I'd lost my mind, but really I'm fine.

It's just me being me.

Now I drive too fast and walk too slow, there's no place special I have to go.

But I don't care, I'm living on a wing and a prayer.

I'll Try Again Tomorrow

I get so wrapped up in daily life I forget to smell the roses. Washing, cleaning, diapers and such, and wiping dirty noses..

The crock-pot book says, fix and forget so this should be a winner. I never turned it on so no surprise, there won't be any dinner.

Washing, cleaning, and errands to run, I keep telling myself motherhood is fun. But the reality is that I can't get ahead, because I'm always behind when I fall into bed.

A new day starts and I promise myself this will be better than the last, then a girlfriend calls to go out to lunch and we reminisce about our past. Who knew parties, dating and love would arrive to throw me out of sync. So what the heck I told myself I might as well have a stiff drink.

Hours later I finally get home to find that no ones even there. But the note on the fridge says they went out to eat, and for once I simply don't care. I went straight to bed without a clear head hoping my thoughts would follow, and I promised myself my new mantra will be, I'll try again tomorrow.

What's Next

We do our daily living and life goes by so fast,
before you know what is today, is actually in the past.

Babies grow to move up and out, while our life made so little change,
but for the ones left behind it's time to consider how to rearrange.

No more nursery room we now have a place for a friend to come visit awhile. We're so glad when they come and yet once they leave it's hard to maintain a smile.

Of being alone and lonely, there are too many people I know, who say they don't have anything, but this is the time to grow.

For something to do that makes you feel good, you offer to volunteer, to do anything, anywhere, any time, any place to eliminate the fear. To find inner peace is the reward that can always be found. Working with others, just look around.

Teachers, dentists, doctors and such, always working, yet doing so much.
To keep us healthy and strong to accept what life will bring.

The best way to enjoy life, just laugh and sing.

The empty nest will be full again, when the children come home with their own.
And you'll smile in your heart as you think to yourself; yes, I have finally grown.

Happy Days

I've done it all up till now; work, children and planting crops in the sun. I'm much older now and want to have fun.

So I leisurely walk in the park, canoe when I can, and ride a bike on the trail. If you believe this you're more gullible than me, for now I'm extremely frail.

Yes, the bones are wearing out and the skin is getting thin, but I'm in great shape, for the shape I'm in.

I spend my days, happily doing jigsaw puzzles I put one together very quickly and then, I take it apart and do it over again.

Some people think it's a game I play; I know it's a job, without any pay. But I do it regardless day after day.

A visit from my children with little ones should always be lots of fun; but I'm working on a puzzle with 1000 pieces and it's already halfway done.

This visit was disastrous right from the start, as they proceed to tip over the table. I move out of the way but not fast enough, and tripped on the internet cable.

Next I see a paramedic looking at me, and checking to see I'm alright. He gives the OK and leaves but did say; check on her throughout the night.

How do I get rid of them so I can get back to work, if I ask them to leave now they'll think I'm being a jerk.

So I go to my room say I'm going to bed, lock up whenever you go, and I jump into bed pretending I'm tired, though this is all for show. Once they're gone I'll get up and go back to work, on the pile of puzzles that started to grow.

Downsizing

I wrote a letter to my children about us moving and their belief that I was glad. I wanted to tell them how I really feel, and that I'm still quite mad.

Dearest Children,

When we moved your dad threw everything out he thought we'd never need. Like a dust pan and broom. Because a man wouldn't use one of those. Out it goes.

Since I was laid up with a broken leg he managed a lot by himself and I'm surprised after moving there's anything left. He simply cleared off every shelf.

Out went my Halloween, Christmas and Easter decor, what would I ever need them for. Also the various kitchen equipment rarely used, like the meat slicer, large griddle, milkshake maker and food mill. All silver and gold items he didn't recognize went in the trash every day, I didn't see it, was never aware, so what could I really say?

Towels and blankets and sheets that were spares, out they went to my despair.

However, tools we'll never use came with us. I'm sure he'll be cutting down trees, and what about the extension ladder, this one put me on my knees!

"Dear God what have I got us into, does he know what apartments are for? Someone else will maintain the upkeep, all we do is sweep the floor. But not anymore. We have no broom, like before."

How could I know what he was doing each day, I was laid up and out of his way. The children all came and asked "What can we do" he said "Load it all up, and take it with you." So they did.

Where are precious memories taken on a camcorder years ago, it breaks my heart to hear him say "The movies? I don't know." Now I have 3 buckets of pictures to go through, that I managed to salvage myself. I'm going through them one by one, before they go back on a shelf.

But he threw out the frying pan from breakfast, he knows I won't make that again.If he doesn't go to Wal-Mart tomorrow, and bring me a baking pan or two; I will either stop eating all together, or I may just move in with you.

With all my love,

Mom

Our New Home

The joys we've had since we first came to be in our brand new home!
It has set us free of yard work and home repairs, and no longer having to pay tax.
On a house with land, school and sewers and no time to ever relax.
The first person we met made us feel right at home and told us of all we could do.
Work out or go shopping, play cards every night, and Bingo much to my delight.
Our pets are welcome, all three dogs and they have adjusted well.
They play like before, and entertain all with the tricks they've been taught..It's swell when they meet other pets, who just like the friends we have made, made them feel right at home.
It's different, that's true, but what a life we lead; doing whatever we desire.
He plays his sports and I write my poems whenever I feel inspired.
These people require very little, but stop and chat for a while.
Then you'll receive the benefit of the gain of a beautiful smile.
So we have enlarged our family and it makes my heart glad to know these people care so.
We've had numerous dinners, served sit-down which my husband loves.
He gets to eat until he's stuffed, then finishes my meal to be sure he's had enough.
Everyone then grabs their baggies and dishes to take the leftovers home.
They really should have asked for more, so they'd have extra to take out the door.
Then they bring on the dessert. I cannot eat another bite.
So I bring it home to have later tonight.
WRONG, it will be gone.
The meals are glorious, I don't have to cook.
I can do puzzles or read on my Nook.
Now I have to go, I'm meeting my ladies in the living room to discuss my latest poetry.
They like to hear it first, so they can be the ones to say;
"Oh that again, I heard it the other day!"

And So We Laughed

Tonight was the worst it's ever been, playing cards with my good friends. We laughed so much I was close to tears, and so shaken with an untold fear of shaming myself by wetting my pants.

We started playing and talking as usual, the compliments were highly paid to the one lady who had joined us late, to the card game she finally made.

It seems she had her hair cut. It was well done and made her look good. So I asked how much she had spent. She said for what, I said the hair cut and this is how it went. "When did you go?" I don't know.How much did you pay? I can't say. Where did you go? I don't remember. And how did you get there?" She said "where?"

This is not the first time I've had this problem, many people here have questionable doubt. They don't know where they've been or who they were with, or if they stayed in or went out. And so we laughed.

I handed a paper to my friend with a joke I had recently told, and she looked so confused. "What's wrong" I said, but I knew in my head what she was going to say. "I didn't ask for this", oh yes you did, so I'll tell you the joke right away." I again told the joke and once more we laughed, for remembering is not their forte, as I looked at the lady who made the request and knew what she was going to say. "Could you please write that down for me, my memory's not what it used to be, so I can tell my friends."

And so we laughed.

Bingo Night

We play Bingo at the home every Wednesday at seven, it's a game of chance. Each board costs a dollar, and it's great when you win and get to holler.
I buy six boards and set them up in the holder that I have.
I get out my water, set myself up and realize I'm really glad.
To be here with my friends enjoying the night as we talk and laugh a lot.
When I yell Bingo, all are glad when they find out the amount I got.
Now winning is fun, but with such a small crowd it shouldn't be done by just one.
We continued to play and a couple girls said how they hadn't won in a while.
I felt so bad when I yelled Bingo again, it was really hard to smile.
We proceeded to play, and I must say, things should have got better.
Finally we're playing the last game of the night which pays the most, and for the third time I raised my hand.
I don't know why I was so lucky, even though I win a lot this was really grand.
We only play ten games, it takes at least an hour and then the split club is played with a gift of cash.
There are six numbers pulled and two colored stubs, one was red and one white.
The last ticket called was my number again and much to my delight,
the evening ended with my final call, as I took the money and said goodnight.
I know tomorrow they'll be talking, and probably ban me from Bingo now,
but they're really fair and they don't care; it's only money anyhow!
So I'll ask before next Wednesday if I'm still allowed to play, if they prefer that I don't it will be fine, I'll just go to the Casino for the day.

Happy Hour

Tonight we had our first Happy Hour, full of laughing and drinking and such.
I had no idea what it was about, or that I'd like it so much.
Each person brought a little snack; and along with it a bottle or two of their favorite smack.
Don't get me wrong, we're entitled to fun and laugh and enjoy every day.
But the Happy Hour Friday's could possible be our downfall in every way.
Since the majority are women who attend our party we share the neatest things.
The conversations, food and the expectation of fun always makes me sing.
No one's aches and pains seem to bother them as they all acted like little kids; much less than sixty.
Could be the wine, or the rum and the coke, for myself mimosas are nifty.
The alcohol flowed for three hours or more, making it hard for some to find the door; not to mention the few who don't know which floor.
But they make it to bed, tomorrow will come, and it will be a better day.
Happy Hour? What do you mean?
Hard to believe they were there and forgot, but that's not really so bad.
If they don't show up next Friday night THAT would be really sad.

Our Director

We have a new apartment director, who is the best of the best. She's the only one to give your thoughts a chance, ready to listen and then skate or dance.

She'll always be there if you need her with an idea or two, and this will always get you through, to where she'll bend and say okay, to the crazy things we do all day.

Like happy Hour. Oh. Yeah. Who wants a bunch of eighty-year-old's, drunk as skunks, hanging around all hours. No. She's smart to say, it's from 4-6 and my shift ends at five.

This is how she stays alive.

She's cute as a bug and smart as a whip; but if she's rattled you may get a grip of her attitude adjusted.

Like in the pandemic when a few stood to gather, she yelled BACK TO YOUR ROOMS, or maybe you'd rather I just say you're all busted.

No more Happy Hour or morning coffee, no poetry reading, or harmony singing. We know what we have and don't want to lose the person who rules this place.

But it all works out, there's happiness here, I can tell as I look at her face. Her name is Patti, she's here for you. When you need her just once, you'll find out how true.

Many Thanks

We live in a place called apartments for seniors, but it's for fifty-five and older. It's kept warm in the winter and now that it's summer, it's starting to feel a little colder.

It's like living in a family or a large commune. If you don't go out they come to your room; making sure you're all right, didn't pass in the night. They all honestly care about each other.

There's planned activities if anyone wants to join in, once a week bingo where you can actually win.

Seasonal holidays are spend having hot dogs and such, and for Mothers and Father's Day there's a big rush, to get to the community room and be first to a table, to sit with good friends when you are able.

The food is delicious; the company superb, the entertainment is funny. Imagine if we had to pay, an evening like this would definitely cost big money.

But we have one person who pulls it all off, she's the one-of-a-kind the management was happy to find.

With one hundred fifty apartments, up to three hundred people to please, it's hard to believe she can accomplish so much.

Give her a thank you, a kind word in passing, offer to help once in a while. The reward is worth it when you get in return, her bright happy face and a smile.

I'm thrilled we're here with all our new friends, there's no better place to be. But I have to end now, because it's time, Nickel Bingo is calling me.

Aging Well

I celebrated another year and all have wished me well,
they'll never know this past year, how I procrastinated like hell.
I realize with the passing time there are things I could have done.
Some for others, or for myself whether it was for work or fun.

I could have climbed a mountain, not just a trail.
I could have won a race or two.
Went horseback riding on a range, or went solo in a plane I flew.

There are many things I'd do over again, and many I'll never admit.
To the husband and children I gave my best part, and so happy to commit,
to the challenge of setting an above par example so they would follow my lead,
I left myself open to give all support with whatever anyone should need.

Now I've celebrated another year and everyone has wished me the best.
They say I've had a great life, enjoyed it to the max, and now I can get some rest.
Are they nuts? This is the time for me to shine.
To never stop laughing and dance until I drop, and maybe stay out after dawn.
This only happens occasionally since by ten I usually yawn.

But I'm changing my life starting now, I won't let my world fill with sorrow.
Another Birthday's gone but I moved along and look forward to tomorrow.

So I'll read the morning paper, and happily see, that on the obituary page there
is no me.
As I rewrite my to-do list, that's the hardest part.
I guess I'll take a little nap, and then maybe I'll start.

Birthday Wishes

It's my birthday today and I'm feeling okay, still can't believe I'm really this old.
Things are so different now.
When I was young I flew through life like a bat.
Laughing and dancing and loving it all, I ponder about all of that.
Rising each day eager to play and never expecting things to change. Suddenly I'm fifty and then I was sixty, then seventy became the new game.
Three quarters of a century, that's where I am and happy to say I'm living up to my name.
I'm not giving up, I've too much to do and a lot to accomplish before I'm through.
So many friends have gone before me; but I make new ones every day.
With my love at my side I'll enjoy my life, saying HAPPY BIRTHDAY to me today.

Today is my Birthday

The 5th of May is my favorite day, it's the day that I was born.
So put on a mask, make a drink, and grab the biggest horn--it's Cinco De Mayo.
We celebrated this way from the time I was a child, as I turned 77 today things took a turn for the mild.
We started our day in the usual way, with breakfast in the community room, at which time they sang Happy Birthday.
I had two Birthday cakes. The one was a work of art; chocolate fudge and delicious.
The cake from my sister had a topper that opened and lit up with about twenty candles. It was glorious.
My daughter made me a BLT as a special request from me, and dinner will be beef stroganoff.
Then on to Bingo tonight to win what we can. This is a big night and I don't care, it's all about winning and not having to share. When we do have to share it's nice to know it's with people where you live and family that you know.
She calls out my number when the split club is done, and this was the second time, oh such fun.
So I've had the best day ever and can gratefully say I'll move on to tomorrow.
With light happy thoughts and love in my heart, I will never know any sorrow.

I Need To Get To Fifty

I'm trying to get to fifty, it shouldn't be hard to write. It seemed much easier a week ago, but then I thought last night.
How hard it is to put to words the thoughts of which I've had, who cares what I think or where I've been, would these make others glad?

To know me is to love me is what the song once said. So here I go; I'll tell you what's inside my head.

I like people who make me smile, babies who giggle a lot, to see a child run and play with their friends always hits the spot.

I like to travel to distant places, but only by reading a book, because boat rides, airplanes and train rides wasted the time it took.

I love cooking and baking for others, to watch them enjoy a good meal.

I enjoy a good game of cards played with my kids. This always makes me feel like we've come a long way to being best friends; not just a Dad and a Mother.
When it's all said and done I have to admit, these feelings are like no other.

I love the Easter egg hunt out in the yard, especially when it was sloppy and wet, They'd dump out their eggs with excitement to see what they finally would get.
Christmas was even better; the house decorated from top to bottom, with gifts galore we'd celebrate more, and baby Jesus wasn't forgotten.

Picnics in the summer, tobogganing in the snow, and for want of something fun to do, off to miniature golf we'd go.

These are just some of my favorite things, everyone has their own too.

It isn't much, but with a touch it's written down to share with you.

Flowers Are For Love

I was given flowers for my Birthday the first part of May and bouquets of roses on Mother's Day. To say I was thrilled, I just couldn't say.
Flowers are an expression of love, they are kissed by the sunshine and rain from above, and handed to me from the children I love.

The personal fragrance of a woman is based on the scent of a flower.

Shampoo, body wash and cologne, too much can overpower.

In a closed area sometimes it can get too heady, like in church next to the woman who bathed in hers, I'd like to have a thought ready.

So how much is too much? I don't really know, I squirt on a little and away I go.

Like the other day after I was ready I used the spray. But when leaving the room I realized I'd grabbed the can of Raid. I didn't think twice, it still smelled nice.It wasn't too bad, with its new floral scent so away I went.

The party was an outside affair, a barbecue in a friends yard. No dressing up, just a social good time; an evening of playing cards.

Three people asked what scent I was wearing they said it seemed familiar. I said it was a new sample bottle and asked for their opinion.

Two said not bad, but prefer my regular and the third said it reminds her of something. Said she'd remember by the end of the night.

It was right at this moment the mosquitoes came out, but I didn't get a bite.

I love my Liz Claiborne and it will still apply when the evening is an affair inside.

But a yard or park, any outdoor event, I'll have Raid along for the ride.

God's Plan

In my mind I walk and run, and often even dance.
I wish I could start over, maybe get a second chance; to sing and dance my way through life as I originally planned.
Now I'm old and tired and thinking, God had a different plan.
He gave me his richest gift, a man to love and children to raise.
We must have done it right as I hear the praise of others who speak so well, of how proud we must be from the poetry that I tell.
It wasn't always easy, sometimes very hard. The washing, cooking and cleaning in a home of fifty years; but we did it with love and loads of sweat and tears.
I thought the house would stand to remind them of their roots.
But God had a different plan.
Moving to an apartment we believed would be grand and now our home no longer stands.
They took it down, leveled it to the ground, but the memories will always remain.
The thoughts of friends and family, all the good and bad times will sustain.
Because God had a different plan.
We we moved on and life is good. We have food to eat and a roof over our head, and new friends and neighbors that are now family, someone said.
Yes I sing when I want, and dance with a little help, but I won't be running anymore.
The last time I tried, I stood there and cried because someone had locked the door.
I wonder sometimes what's on His mind, and where do we go from here.
We'll just go on and follow His plan and do it without any fear.
It no longer matters if I run, dance or sing; I could be happy to patiently sit.
Because where I am is where He wants me to be and I have to admit - I like it.

God Changed the Plan

I haven't written in quite a while, so I put pen in hand to make me smile.
We've been through a lot in the last few months, first the Corona thing and Howie's emergency surgery; when I broke down and I lie when I say everything is okay.
I was just trying to get through every day.
Seems my heart couldn't handle the mess.
Thank God we have children and enough to go around, that they covered the hours of food, medications and such.
Never complaining when what we asked for was too much.
They were raised with love and a strong gentle hand, and they gave it back to us when God changed the plan.
Our oldest son came in for the first two weekends and slept sitting on the couch.
I'm sure by the second one his wife is saying "Don't go back you're a serious grouch."
One daughter alone kept all three dogs, a job I truly admire since she just got a dog of her own.
It's been two and a half months so when they came home today it was with tears of joy.
She brought their dog dishes, all their food, and each and every toy.
This will entail a scheduled walk twice a day with Howie and the dogs
One girl was in charge of his medications and organized all that he took.
She also scheduled our meals from each day and wrote them in a book.
The bills we dealt with were looked at by one who works with the system everyday.
So she checks them out to be certain we don't have to pay.
Then there are the best times, when we all get together for dinner and cards.
We laugh and joke and simply enjoy the company of each other.
Husband and wife, sisters and brother.
I wish they could all be here but Corona ended that, so I'll call the others later and we'll have a terrific chat.
We are blessed and we know it, without a doubt, it gives us a reason to always shout.
I love you so much, you are vital to me; if my time ended now how grateful I'd be.

Before It's Too Late

To live to see, to be and do, all the things God meant for you.
You never know what is your final date, say it now before it's too late.
Tell someone how much you care, not just a few quick words.
Say what's truly in your heart, and don't be afraid to be heard.

The gift of life is precious, how much more time do you have to give love to another.
In religion we're taught to love one another, at home we are taught to be guarded.
Which is it then, do we love all strangers, and how do I get started.
To right this wrong I will be strong, and show love to everyone I know.Without a doubt
I'll leave someone out, that I really shouldn't miss.
And there are a selected few who'll also get a kiss.

How hard can it be to be nice, to all the folks you greet every day?
Or to speak the words? Just tell them so, here's what you can say.
Hey, I had a thought of you today, it was warm and fuzzy. Did you feel it too? If you
didn't that's okay, I often think of you.
Now leave it there and walk away; and someday soon you'll find, that someone says it
back to you, and you'll think, "That was kind."

Believe

I wash the floors on hands and knees as my mother always said.
I cook and iron and clean, when I'd rather be comfortable in bed.
What's wrong with me, I ask myself, what is it I require?
To be respected and loved by everyone is my greatest desire.
All people need kindness in life; each person needs to know,
everyone is special, so be sure to tell them so.
A stranger is a friend you haven't met yet!
Be willing to take a chance, do not judge who they are, or what they are like by just a very quick glance.
A person may be lonely and not asking for much, but a kind word or two would be a warm touch.
Have you helped some one out with kindness and grace?
Can you see how this puts a smile on your face?
So walk in the sunshine, look them straight in the eye, say "I'm here for you now."
Give it a try.
In no time at all I know I will achieve the respect I require, because I believe.

Days of Yore

I long for the days when I was a child, when people were kind and thoughts were mild.
When it didn't matter who or what you believe.
You could ride your bike through the neighborhood and not worry of who you would meet.
Visit your friends and play all day until the lights came on in the street.
We had no pool in the summer to swim in, we'd run under the garden hose.
And sometimes we used it for drinking, not worried about a bug up our nose.
The neighbors all knew us, and we knew them, they were from all walks of life.
Fruit vendors, doctors, tradesmen and yet, there was one especially I'll never forget.
He owned the funeral parlor on our street, a nicer family you'll never meet.
His kids were the best of them all. I would baby-sit them and I don't like to boast, but the day did come when I met a ghost.
We had a local playground one street away and down a block the children would play.
There were kids from everywhere black, yellow and white and they all got along.
They'd be splashing and playing and burst into song yelling Marco Polo to each other.
These were the best times and we'd never expect the world would change so much.
The times they are so different now, smart phones and the internet make me feel out of touch.
The important thing is for people to connect, not as a message but as a telephone call.
See them, feel them, give them a big hug and a kiss.
For a hug one gets back is truly pure bliss.
Show people you care, put your phones down, and enjoy the meal you are eating.
You may be surprised by what you hear, and this requires repeating.
Put down your phone. Nothing is more important than who is with you right now and this change will surely grow.
Tell everyone that you're doing your part to have them listen with their heart.

Respect

I tried so hard to teach them right. That there are more things in life than money.

Pride in yourself as your journey goes on, you must laugh at yourself since it's funny.
How the road will change when you least expect and go quickly from gloomy to sunny.

Lend a hand when you can to lighten someone's load, be sincere and always be kind.
Be truthful, honest and sincere when you speak then surely you will find.

Respect is earned, one will finally learn by being true to yourself. Live a good life and
no one will fail to show you respect above all else.
Its not what you say, it's how it is said, this I was taught by my mother. So speak softly
and clearly, encourage your own to do the same for others.

Respect will come if you show it first, this I truly believe. We teach our children morals
and manners hoping to find the respect they achieve.

Don't brag or bully as you go through life, the journey is way too short. To leave paths
of destruction behind you won't give feelings of high self-worth.

To have people say at the end of the day, it was great knowing him or her.

To finally realize as you detect, you've actually earned their deep respect.

If I Could Be A Better Me

I'd like to go where I would be in a place of perfect harmony where I could be a better me.

A place with faults so few that no one knew of the person I was or how, a new door opened and I walked through, to be where I am now.

Where I could be a better me.

Though times are tough and life gets rough, we all need to smile and see.

That being happy or sad is a choice we make, to be a better me.

So I listen to others and laugh and sing to help them to be happy too.

That in time I just know it will prove itself, I can be better too.

Eternity

Eternity is a very long time, so just say you'll love me right now.

Scholars say true love is felt, when your heart beats like a drum, when your breath is taken away by the words that are said, and your whole body seems to be numb.

Love is an emotion, a feeling of goodness, faith and peace of mind.

A safety net when the storm clouds come and leave us feeling less kind.

Love is gentleness and patience is what we were taught.

Love is trust and respect, and never a vile thought.

These are all things that occur over a lifetime, now you say eternity to me.

I believe you speak truly from your heart without any intent to deceive.

Now I'll ask you to say you'll always love me, with a goal that we both can achieve.

But eternity; that's a long time away, so for right now I'll simply say. "Not for a month or a year, but for a lifetime as my lover and friend, I'll love you and hold you to it, until your very end."

Family

What is considered a family, if not the people you live with and see each and every day.
It's people you greet as you come and go, and pass in the halls on your way.
It's sharing a smile and a hearty "Hello" as you quickly run on by.
Or a sit-down and chat session filled with concern over something that's making them cry.
Family doesn't mean you are directly related, but because you both care
In the feelings you share the friendship never ends.
Who would believe that in their seventies people start making new friends.
Let me tell you the truth, it happens daily if you just get up and go.
We moved to our new place and I now have 93 new friends.
I believe that everyone needs other people in their life, to swap stories or share good and bad news, and challenge others to speak their mind.
That's what social interaction is.
It's my opinion that everyone needs people, some not as much as others;
but to not care what your neighbors are needing isn't treating them like brothers.
So sit and talk, or walk a bit with them, and you'll find as you go.
A little tremor will start in your heart and you'll say, "This is a friend I'd like to know.
Before you know the list will grow and you've turned their life around.
Then one sunny day you'll realize, it was you who was turned around.

My Dear Child

It's 6 a.m. and I can't sleep, too many thoughts running through my head. Since 2 a.m. I've thought about you and wished you were here instead.

You're so far away so all I can say is I'm thinking of you today.

It makes me glad for the short time we had as you grew up and out of my life. I worry so about where you are, and that your world may be full of strife.

Be calm my love, be happy and free until your world gives you back to me.

I love our short talks and the visits you make as they again refill my heart with your love.

And a prayer goes up to keep you safe as He watches you from above.

Just know that a mother's love can never be lost, it's an unbreakable chain, and when you're back home, the hug that you get will prove it to you once again.

With Love,

Your Mother

My Garden

My garden grows with beautiful flowers, a type you've never seen.
It's not that I won't share them, that isn't what I mean.
I keep them cool or warm depending on the day and feed them what
they ask for.
For they're delicate creatures and one of a kind that can't be found in
any store.
They're blonde haired and blue eyed, and brown eyed with curls.
They're known as my grandchildren, all diamonds and pearls.
They use imagination and talk of growing up, which happens way too soon.
And just like the flowers in my garden, they all begin to bloom.
First there's preschool than grade and high school, where they all
equally excel.
They fill my world with more hugs and kisses than I can ever tell.
Then comes college and working with passion at a job they simply love.
And I watch them grow older with blessings, granted from high above.
They go through their days with a constant smile, now they meet someone special and
they walk their way down the aisle.
So, I'm back in my garden again, as I look at the new plant I just found.
Thanking God that for once I was ready, and because He let me stay around. A new
generation, a new life to mold, and now a great-grandchild to lovingly hold.
To know them, to love them, for the time that I'm given, this is my garden and I'm
thankful I'm living.

Family Retreat

Children are such a blessing to you, they have grown up and given us so many memories.
I guess it was time to make more.
So our daughter found a place that would take all of us with our dogs and so…we went on a four day vacation.
It was nothing like we had ever done.
All 21 of us together and ready for four days of fun.
Each family was assigned a meal so we only ate the best, but after eating they couldn't seem to rest.
Grabbing a kayak, paddle board or canoe, and tried to do what they thought they could do.
They were huffing and puffing, all out of breath. Stuffed from eating but what the heck!
I looked around and watched them all moaning and groaning and making terrible sounds.
After a time they assembled around the volleyball net, it was high on a hill.
I couldn't see them, but I could hear them all picking on the oldest brother.
They spent the evening sitting around telling stories and relating to each other.
Just like that everyone said goodnight and ten minutes later I awoke with a fright, as I heard HALLWAY, HALLWAY, HALLWAY as they ran.
This became a nightly mantra .And I never tired of hearing it.
Jordyn and Peyton would lead the group followed by the adults, stamping and yelling.
These are the stories they'll be retelling.
It was a short week of togetherness that meant so much to the two that started it all.
We thank you all for it.

A Shopping Day

Today was fun with my daughter, we spent hours at the store. Looking for
summer clothes to replace those I currently wore.
I had a considerable weight loss and no longer did anything fit, beside
the fact they went back to 1980 when I'd originally bought all of it.

So we hunted the aisles of three department stores looking for what I'd like,
for an evening of dress-up, or gardening and such, or just lying around the house, and
the jeans I'd need for picnics and things, or taking a ride on my bike.

We go to check out and the bills not so bad, it came to around 300 dollars.
I count out my money and I start to pay when, "Mother are you crazy!" she hollers.
We should go elsewhere, where things cost less and you can get more for your money.

I say "No thanks, these are much better made, but thanks for worrying honey."
She seems quite mad as we leave the store, and I think I have to find out more.

So I offer to buy her lunch. "Oh no" she says, "I'll wait for dinner." This I didn't expect.
Come on I said, it's my treat, today I get my check. I know, she says with her lips
pinched tight. She's worried about my bank account, I was right.
Now here goes another fight.

Don't worry honey, my money is saved for you, it'll be there when I'm gone.
But right now I want to spend time with you, it's what I've wanted all along.
I really needed this clothing you know, as mine no longer fit.
Lunch is just to keep you with me until you say"I quit" and take me
back to the home, where I'll wander alone or just find a chair and sit.

She cried when I told her, never knowing how sad and lonely I'd become.
She sped back to my place, loaded everything up, and I now have a new home.
I should have told her long ago, I just didn't want to complain.
Still we talked it out and made a plan, when I become senile and old
and have to go she'll explain.
I love having you with me day to day,it breaks my heart to give you away.,
But you'll see we'll both have a much better day.

Can't Stay

I open the door and my heart stands still as I look at you standing there.

You've grown into a man so beautiful and suave without a worry or care.
After high school and the Army, you moved far away, you wanted to travel
far and wide.

You were happy alone going along, with no friend at your side.

You had many friends, but happily they knew you'd be gone again, nothing stopped
you.

This is the way you always were and everyone already knows, you won't
be here long when you hear your song calling from far away.

So sit down lets talk before you walk, I wish to hear what you say.

You start with your travels, you've been far and wide, seen things that others don't
know. How bad are some lives, people gnarled from life, but smiling all the day.

You say it's hard to recall where you've been after all, it's been so many years.

You're here now and ready to stay. To be around a long while should make me smile,
but I say something you don't want to hear.

Welcome home I'm so glad you came, you can move back into your old room, but I'm
sorry to say I'm not able to stay.

For it won't be very long when I'll be hearing my song.

Hand In Hand

It was so much fun when I was young to walk holding hands with my guy.
I was proud he was mine and with our two hearts combined, our love would grow richer with time.
We were lovers and friends before we became a husband and wife.

The whole world shifted and enlarged as we started a married life. Many children were born so he worked overtime to give us what he thought we deserved. Missing out on his newborns he gave it all up to watch them grow as he observed. Childhood's too short he'd always say; I want to be the first and last thing they see every day.

So he'd come home from work; get down on his knees and play with the babies a while. Then head out with the others to take a bike ride, always wearing a quirky smile. Awesome Dad, they all said with pride in their hearts as they listened to stories he told; of growing up as a boy with so much less, letting them know just how much they were blessed. He was strict and gentle, a little crazy at times, always fun to be around.

When thinking about his heart many things I have found. Waking each day with a smile on his face has been a constant reminder, that he forgives with his heart those who've hurt him and starts every single day being kinder. He dances with no rhythm, sings way off- key; but these are the dearest things to me.

Helping neighbors, strangers, family, friend, doesn't matter the request, he'll do what he can to help anyone out, and always give it his best.

So we reminisce and talk as we casually walk, speaking of our life beneath the moon. But still holding hands I think to myself that life goes by way too soon.

And I realize as we walk I can finally relax. This guy that I've loved for all these years has filled my heart to the max.

You Are Amazing

You are an amazing incredible person, every day you take my breath away. By the things you do and what you say, an outpouring of love always coming my way.

You make the skies sunny on a cloudy day, and the stories you tell in your funny way are what make me love you.

The way you treat others so quietly caring, about how they are or have been. Speaks volumes about you, how gentle you are, and that you'd give your life for a friend.

You have determination and stamina when things seem unsure of any ending in sight., You plod on through and just keep on until everything is right.

To know you is to love you I always tell others. And they know that once you've met, it's truly hard not to like you and once that's done you're impossible to forget.

Good looking and suave you tell jokes like a pro, you're always kidding around. But not always when you talk to me, I get a better sound.

I love your voice as you send sweet words my way, and vow your love forever and a day. Thank you is all that I can say.

All of Me

What would I do if I didn't have you?
You are every emotion I've felt.
You are the love of my life, the summer of my heart.
You're the quiet in my mind when I'm trying for peace.
from the buzzing in my head.
You fill my head with joy for the inane things you do to make me smile.
You're always on top of things. Bring out the best in others as well as yourself.
You're an amazing man I wish I could be more like you.
You should have been a President, everyone would work with you.
You're straightforward and always caring about the other guy, never in yourself.
You're an amazing piece of work and God broke the mold.
He shouldn't have, he could have ruled the world with legions of you.

My Love

How can I tell you how much I love you? There are no words to be said.

I've loved you forever and always will until the day I'm dead.
But, I'll love you more after and until we meet again, in a place no one can find.
Our bodies will be gone, but the soul lives on, and you will be on my mind.

In our younger years it was dating and fun. Then as time went on we two became one.
The joys of friends and family and a home that we bought, to fill with the laughter of
children was what we both thought. Would be the next step in our well planned life.
You did the work, with a stay-at-home wife.

You have given me comfort and care in a life that can be so rough.
You've managed to smile through the worst times, your spirit is so tough.
That you just love me regardless of all my worldly faults is amazing to me.
That after all this time you think I'm fine, and suddenly I see.
What we started years ago, when we were very young, not knowing
how our love would survive.
Yet here we are so many years later, and it still continues to thrive.

So I'll give you love today and all my days to come, and when He finally calls me home
I'll be waiting just for you.
And with a smile in my heart as you hold me tight, I'll say again "I love you."

Dogs Vacation

Our dogs are on vacation staying overnight with Aunt Janine.
She kindly offered to watch her sister's pet but it was unforeseen.
That if you do for one you do for all, and since we do have three,
I thought it time to get a break and have my place be free.

Of toys and beds, and dishes besides; the constant walks and many car rides.
The bathing, brushing, and feeding and such, who would believe it takes so much.
To say they aren't happy would be a lie, as they happily play all day.
To protect, love us are what they were told as their breeder gave them away.
So, they do their job and with warm eyes that smile as they accept all my praise.

But I thank God for Janine who took them away so I could have empty days.

Well I look forward to this week without any dogs. They'll be no commands of down, sit,
or stay, no drooling over my meal. No time-outs in their dog beds when they refuse to
heel.

She says they'll be messy when she brings them back home, but not to worry she has
both brush and comb.
They will be happy and wild coming back to our place; bundles of energy I'm sure. But
the thing I know is they will miss me so, and will look at me with love so pure.

Now I think to myself as long as I'm alive and she can survive, maybe we could make a
plan. To do this more often, like maybe each week or as often as she can.

The Puppy

I looked up with fear as he drew near, she was so meek and mild.
When I was bigger I'd let him know he could no longer hurt this child.
For now all I was able to do was growl and try my best, to stop his anger before it came to rest on the little one in my care.

My mother told me as I left her side, that a dog's life is one of pride.
To take care of their owner, be patient and kind, and never let anyone hurt them. My mother gave me to them never knowing that he would be the kind of person he turned out to be. Always cursing and yelling and forever telling how he wanted peace and quiet, what did he expect with a new baby around? So I stood my ground.

I bit him once and his boot hit my ribs, but I didn't stop my advance.
I knew she needed me to deter him, or she didn't have a chance.
My mother was right, so for me to be proud I did what I had to do. I'd fight him each time and the pain I'd receive was one more she wouldn't get, though I'm bruised and sore it matters no more.

By the time she was five he finally died. I was thrilled she would grow and finally know that people could be kind.

She's all grown now with children of her own and a better mother there never could be. As for me I'm proud, I took the blows and no one knows, how devoted she was to me. She always said thank you and that she loves me, of that I have no doubt. She cuddles me close I wish I could speak for then I'd be able to shout as I cried, Mother was right a dog's life is his pride.

Trying to Quit

I'm in a room for quitters, trying to be positive and gay.
So I listen to the one man show, to hear what he has to say.
He speaks of personal rewards and goals we set for oneself.
The health that is going to improve, and what we're not spending in time will bring us great wealth.
I've tried hypnosis, that didn't work. But If I rub my ears, I do relax.
I did try Chanex.
It wasn't bad, but the nightmares were really scary.
So it's the same old thing and it won't be easy.
The last time I tried, for three weeks I cried.
What made me think this time would be breezy?
I find day to day I think about it more, and it's really driving me crazy.
I'd been a girlfriend, mother, a friend and a wife.
I started at thirteen and it's been a great life, puffing all the way.
Now I'm older, no wiser, not smoking right now.
The place where I live it is not allowed.
I no longer drive; can't get to the store, but I so do want to smoke once more.
They say use the gum, but it sticks to my teeth and pulls my denture out of place.
My grandson saw me and yelled, that's a terrible look on your face.
I put on fifteen pounds and need new clothes; all this weight has finally come to rest.
I've spread out everywhere, my hips and my thighs, but not even one inch on my chest.
I'm tired and listless, not happy to be me, and the rage that often surfaces is not the real me.
I'll keep trying until I get it right, so someday I can say, "I won the fight".
It'll all pay off as an example to my kids, when I live those extra years.
But I'd rather say, screw it and have a smoke instead of crying more tears.

Cancel the Wedding

I need to eat something sweet at least once a day. You know how it goes. You're running late and so a couple of cookies will do.

You grab two on the run, it should have been one, you return now and take quite a few.

You get to work, call yourself a jerk, for you've eaten your sweets for the day, Your co-worker comes in with donuts for all, so you head for the box right away.

The lunch hour comes and you're ready to run, to the restaurant just up the street. A sandwich and soup, with pie for dessert would be, ever so sweet.

Now you're up five extra pounds. You won't fit in the dress you need to wear down the aisle. So you head for the gym and work out for an hour, and by this time, can no longer smile.

This is not good for your body; the binge has got to stop. You're falling apart over a dress, it's the wedding you have to drop.

You tell your boyfriend there will be no wedding, he laughs and asks you why." Cause I'm gaining weight and my dress won't fit," and then you start to cry. "No worry," he says "we'll just elope; no one will know any better. It's not in the paper, invitations aren't ordered, and no one has gotten a letter."

You tell yourself this is good, you can relax and stop overeating. But it is okay to once a day, do a little cheating.

Depends

I wear Depends and nobody knows, I can wet myself and it doesn't show. This simply means, I don't have to say "I need a bathroom right away!"
The joy of being out for a night, with my daughters and sisters to laugh and dance was the thought of a dream come true.
But nothing compared to the outcome, since I ended up black and blue.
This is how it happened: I started to dance and tripped on my oxygen cord, not a good start at all.
I broke my nose when my face hit the floor. Getting up on my feet I peed my Depends, I thought isn't this great after all.
So I head for the ladies room to clean up my mess, looking at myself in the mirror I can't believe what I see.
My nose is bleeding I'm all black and blue and no one came in to help me. These are my sisters and daughters. Looking in the mirror behind me I see what stopped them for sure, my pants are split and the Depends then dropped all the way to the floor.
I asked the laughing waitress running by if they had a back door, "Sure we do honey, this is what we keep it for."

Man's Invention

A man once looked at his woman and said, "ah ha" I have to make a bra.
Something to hold her up and keep her looking right, or maybe even more sensual on a given night.

It had to be a man, no woman would say. Bind me up I like it that way.
We've come a long way since the first invention, and the newest models make it look like perfection.

They all come with wires to support a heavy load, woe to the girls who have a long way to go to fill them out. Then they are nicely padded to give a larger view of the bust that needs a lift or two.

The women who've had enlargements are sad. If they'd only waited they could have had the same look they paid for, just to have more.

A few years back women tried to prove a point by burning their bras which didn't go over too well. Now it costs so much to look like everyone else it's often too hard to tell, are they real or a fake, just give it a break. These things designed by a man are strictly for their enjoyment, so it's fair to let them wear them.

Now I'm working on something to help a man with his package that should make all the ladies smile. I'll wrap them up with a wire lift and padding, so we can see them for a mile.

Lists

Yes I write lists, more of them than I need.

A list for groceries, a list for food, one for each recipe I cook.

This takes me to the list I have for all my baking books.

Then to the list for what to read, add to the list I've read,

Then add those to the list to delete, because now these books are dead.

On to the address list to post the mail, and check on the Internet.

Someone has moved, now I need to find my password list to connect.

My to-do list gets longer everyday, and I threaten to throw it out.

But I'd be lost without it, wouldn't know where to go or how to

plan my day no doubt.

I have a list of my cousin's names, for when they come to lunch.

And a larger one for their family picnic, when I call for the whole bunch.

Then there's the grandchildren's list for school functions that I get to attend with a

smile.

I go to these things thinking, as a grandmother should, "I've gone the extra mile".

God forbid my husband asks for food like making his favorite dish,

I look at him like he's going crazy and say "I'll put it on the wish list".

Something About Nothing

I have a thought in here but it's not clear, whatever it's going to be. It starts and ends so quickly I fear this is how it's meant to be.

One moment it's there and then it's gone, when did my brain get so bland? I begin to write now the thought is gone, I just don't understand.

With age comes wisdom a wise person once said, but I don't believe that's true, at least it's not for me, maybe it is for you.

I write it down so I won't forget, only to misplace the note. But it's not real important whatever it was, because I can't find what it is I wrote.

Now I go with great speed to finally read, and then the thought finally sank. As I laugh to myself when I look at the paper, and find that it's really just blank.

Poetry

Why is it, I said, that each thought in my head turns out to be a rhyme?

I think of a word and how absurd again it rhymed this time.

Just once I'd like to write a note that doesn't rhyme at all.

Then I read it through and feel as though I've already dropped the ball.

Now I write a line I'm doing fine, it's going along quite well.

It was until I read it through and thought oh what the hell.

There's something strange inside my brain, making me do what I do.

I think it's pretty funny, that the thought in my head is the next thing that I say should either be honey or sunny.

Now I'll just quit because it's ridiculous, this problem I'm fighting about.

I can't change, the words just rearrange and poetry comes tumbling out.

Troubled Thoughts

Some days I find it's hard to write my poetry and have it rhyme.
When I think of a subject to speak of, and not just to waste my time.
I've written about mothers and children; morals, respect and love, growing up, growing old, friendship and more.
Some poems were stories and others just a thought, so I put it on paper and that's when I read the thoughts that I couldn't get out of my head.
Of the old man who is lost, or the daughter who is missing, and of all the people in need.
I read the paper and wish I could help the family whose house burned and left them without shelter and food. With little children this is not good. They have no place to go, no money to spend on a room or hotel, when does it end.
There are animals abandoned by someone so mean, they weren't fed or sheltered, and never kept clean.
If we don't start to show that we really do care, how will our youngsters learn anywhere that this is our job, our responsibility.
One's lifetime is short to do all that needs to be done. To shape up the world and still have fun. But it can be done.
If every day we do one good deed, like donate a coat or a dinner to someone in need.
Or maybe just listen to someone's pleas of a better way for you and me.
The quality of life isn't what you you have. It's what you put into it.
So put yourself out there, give til it hurts, overextend yourself.
In no time at all you'll feel an immense sense of satisfaction, that started as just a tiny idea and has become your main attraction.

Senior Benefits

We've moved on in our journey as husband and wife, after so many years and a wonderful life.

We're told senior apartments are where we will end, and this place is great where I've made many a friend.

The age we're at gives us so much more, there's Medicare, AARP and discounts galore. You can also ask for senior discounts at almost every store.

With hearing aids, dentures, and walkers in our home, we have every device we need when we decide to roam.

To play cards when we want, watch TV night and day, there's an exercise room when we just want to play.

We can have meals on wheels and medications rushed in; there are alarms in the rooms to bring the paramedics in.

Thank God it wasn't later when we got the call. But needless to say, we now have it all.

Shopping on the Internet

If you haven't shopped on the Internet, you're missing all the fun.

I don't have to get dressed, because I won't meet anyone.

The prices are great, there are no closing hours, and they deliver right to my door.

Now instead of a local minimum tax I pay shipping charge equal to that. But they deliver it to my door.

Comparing the prices to other sites is easy enough; I make my selection and pay. I get a confirmation code and I'll have it right away.

Well, not really, 7-10 days is the usual time, rarely is it longer. But, they deliver right to my door.

Do not be concerned if the item doesn't fit or if you decide you no longer need it, you can easily return it.

Call the company back and ask for the code to ship your item back to the store.

This should only take a minute but after the first 4 hold buttons and one hang up I said I can't take anymore. Finally someone helpful answers and gives me what I need.

I wrap it right and drive to the post office with speed. It needs to be stamped today's date or I lose a 25% restocking fee. The cost to return is $13.95, he can't be talking to me.

I only paid $19.99 plus shipping; I'm already at $41.53. This is not including the restocking fee!

But, I didn't get dressed or meet anyone and they brought it right to my door.

Just Another Day

Just a little ditty because I'm feeling kind of witty with the voices running rampant in my head. Not sure if it'll go anywhere and really I don't care, because I can always bake a cake or some bread.

It does seem kind of silly, when I'm feeling Willy-nilly, like that's when I have so much to say. So I'll get right to it, and right on through it, before my brain shuts down for the day.

I'm up at seven and headed for the pot, the coffees perking and the thirst that I got, was quenched with my first sip. I knew I'd regret it, it was really too soon, as I scalded my fat bottom lip.

I moved to the basement for the first load of wash, forgetting to put in the bleach.

Stretching up for the same, using His name in vain as it spilled when it fell from my reach.

My dogs are all dirty from their first morning run, to do their thing before they can eat. Now it's baths for all three, then one for me since now I don't smell very sweet.

Rushing out of the room, I tripped on the broom,and landed spread out on the floor.

I need a break I tell myself, as I sit there trying to unwind, I don't think I can take anymore.

Now I say to myself "I'll just take a walk" but starting to leave I find, if I don't make some changes in the days of my life, I'm going to be out of my mind.

There will be no more clean clothes,or my words of prose, and maybe that will be that.

Cause I'll be rid of the house and also the dogs and trade them all in for a cat.

Carried Away

I haven't felt like writing too much, my days are too mundane.

I'm drowning in reading on my Nook, and playing video games.

To beat my score I try for more, and end up farther behind.

Then I read a little then read it again, before I simply find.

My brain has frozen in time and space, and I can't see the

words in front of my face.

I really do feel out of place, this whole day has become a disgrace.

So I'm up and out of bed with a plan to get something done.

Should I wash or clean, or bake something?

Which would be more fun?

I pace back and forth,but today I'm really slow.

Three more chapters I'm done, so back to bed I go.

Something I noticed in writing today, my thoughts really

got carried away.

Babies Are Adorable

I used to say, babies are so adorable, soft and warm and sweet.

Move on ten years, give them a bike and send them out in the street.

You can tell they're teens from the way that they dress,dirty old jeans and their shirt is a mess.,

Hair that's not brushed; do they even own a comb.

I can't believe he's mine when he finally does come home.

He aced it in college, I just knew he'd go far.

He's now the head mechanic to work on any car.

He moves on with his life and finds a sweet wife, and the two finally become three.

In thinking over his lifetime I realized, that was so like me!

Now I say, it's deplorable that babies are so adorable.

I'm Getting Older

I used to hold your hand as we walked in the park, then I'd hold you tight when things scared you in the dark.

Now it's my turn to be scared, but I try not to show, how worried I am and can't let go, of the life I treasure so.

I would yell "Don't run you'll fall," but back then you didn't care, you'd say "No pain no gain."

Now I move too fast and "Mother" you shout, " Remember to use your cane."

We go out to lunch and meet up with friends, this is such a treat. But, I'm embarrassed to hell with the napkin round my neck, you put there to help me eat.

I'm your mother not your daughter, remember to treat me as such. You learned things before, you can do it again. I'm not really asking too much.

To be able to run is a long ago thing, just pushing a walker the memories it brings, of chasing after children laughing and playing . These were the best times.

And now I'm saying. Hold my hand cause we're friends not like my mom, be supportive and kind and true. To the manners and morals I spent years, teaching all this to you.

To give up for elders,table manners and such, these are the things that meant so much, to me as a teacher taught with a steel glove. So you'd give to others an abundance of love.

Do it for me now it's my turn to shine. And I'll be so grateful child of mine.

Senior Living

We've moved on up in our journey through life, with so many years as husband and wife.

They say senior apartments are where we all will end; but it's not too bad this place where we live, in fact I've made many a friend.

This is the result of staying too long in only one house all the time.
There's so much to go through, what to keep or throw out, either way it's really a crime.
That we saved all the pictures and videos and such, to keep as the memories evade.
Knowing others don't remember how important it is that these thoughts don't ever fade.

We moved in with the minimum and said it was more than enough, no words were ever more true.
What more do we need than a bed and t.v., no more kids it's just me and you.

There's a gym to work out, a room to make friends, and three libraries just for reading.
We play Bingo on Wednesday, chair Yoga each morning, poker every afternoon.
Parties for birthdays with cake and ice cream and at 100 you get a balloon.

Now this is where I'll spend my life, writing and listening to their stories.
The stories are varied and good for comparing to how great my life has been.

We've had ups and downs but you've never failed to show me you're still my best friend.
Now we're here to stay so I can only say, thank you again for every day.

Medicare and Me

Today I need my medicine, it's not as easy as you think. After the day I've had today, I know why people drink.

I can't get my medications anymore, the company no longer exists. My breathing is shorter and so is my life, I'm having a problem with this.

I spent the morning calling for alternate ways to get a prescription to me. Not asking for much and happy to pay, I don't expect it's for free.

I call the resource department at my husbands work; they gave me our insurance number to call. I thought this was quite a perk. Until I realized the insurance lady did the same, and just gave me Medicaid's number, the jerk.

Now I'm put on hold until she works it out, and feel like I'm getting somewhere. After ten minutes waiting I look at the phone and now no number is there.

My battery went down how would I know, I have to call them back and here we go. I start all over and take it slow. So I dial once more and I'm on hold, for them to do whatever they can. To provide me with medicines for the rest of my life, this is the overall plan.

We spend our days working, to better our lives and be happy and live pain free. It only took an hour and a half, and six phone calls later to get back to me being me.

Ms. Mohammed, as I write this today, you saved me time and tears. Now when the medicine comes I can seriously say, thank you for my additional years.

My Mother

There is only one other person I know who could make me believe in myself,

and helped me grow like no other. This person of virtue grace and love is none other than my Mother.

Her voice so sweet and always strong, was a welcome sound to my ear. Be it joking or criticism, it was done with love in a song. High soprano for good, and loud bass for wrong.

She taught me manners and respect, cleanliness and such. She knew everything and I loved her so much.

She's been gone for awhile and I do miss her smile. It was a good day for me when she'd call and say, "Would it be okay to stop over?" I'd say "Yes, please do," and with a beer or two, she'd be there with no delay.

Yes she had problems of her own that she never shared with me. She was only concerned with how I had been, that I was content with the life I had, and I didn't think to ask her, "When was she last glad for what she had?"

She never griped or complained, yet life took her down and she was gone in the blink of an eye.

Will I see her again? Will I be her friend or will she still be my Mother?

I'd like it to be both but it doesn't really matter, I'll be glad for one or the other.

Mother's Rules

I told my husband the day we wed that I was his wife, not his child.
He could take care of me, but not boss me around and he looked at me and smiled.
I went from a daughter to being a wife and never believed for the rest of my life he was in charge of me.

I would be wife and mother and need to know he would agree with the way we raised our children. This is a very tough job. We agreed a large family was what we want, but they wouldn't turn into a dangerous mob He said do it your way and I will say nothing unless it's too strong. Than together we'll figure how to right a wrong. I believed I was fair, firm, and strict when I punished a child. Sassing or lying got soap in their mouth and a spanking was never mild. But they grew up happy and secure knowing they were loved.

We bought a house to raise a family this was a very large step.
We furnished it with many a nice thing, but not very expensive knowing the children would bring havoc and mayhem; destruction galore.
With five children in six years and years later, two more.
They were actually very well behaved at least when we'd go out. I had a look that would stop them in their tracks, I never had to shout.

There were only two rules in their younger age. You must follow the golden rule, so if they did bad to others, I did bad to them, and that would make them think about doing it again. The other was table manners, with a strong heavy hand.
I said napkins in your laps, and wasn't it grand, how they'd pick up their arm since it wasn't too heavy, to put food in their mouth when they were ready.
To go out to eat was always a treat as we didn't do it often, but the waitress always asked if when we came back, she would be requested, said it was a pleasure to see so many kids and nobody getting arrested.

I joined the women's auxiliary for our volunteer firemen, worked the bingo and catered weddings; this was all for fun.
Took me out of the house and away from it all and I have to admit I had a ball!
I'd win a little money or earn a little bit, but it was a night out for myself and I was loving it.

The children are raised now with babies of their own and I hope we've taught them well.
And though we're out of that house, the memories are swell. There were tears of joy and sorrow, days of giggle and fun, but it must be said it can't be done by one.
It takes two at their top speed to keep it in line and we did it as one, every single time.

Mother

Many try to explain what a Mother is, so I'm going to give it a go.

She's a person first, a very young girl, with dreams and ideals.

She gives of herself and expects nothing back, this is how she feels.

She's a caregiver and nurse, a waiter and a maid, a porter, a chauffeur

and a preacher.

She's a psychologist, a nanny, baker and cook.

She sings babies to sleep, and could easily write a book.

But she's soft and pure and full of love.

God designed her to be all things, for she is like no other.

He made her delicate with the biggest heart and then he named her, MOTHER.

The Game

I remember when I was just a child my mother would come into my room.
We'd play a game on the floor, this was such a good time for me that I've longed for it evermore.
We'd get silly and laugh and laugh til our sides would hurt, but I couldn't enjoy it more.

Then the day would change as I grew up and my mother came no more.
With three other siblings and taking care of our needs she didn't have time for a game.
Cooking and cleaning, making our clothes, she wasn't the one to blame.

I missed the time we spent together and soon I was an adult.
With my own family now I watched her age and found it was my fault. She was lonely and sad and always so glad that I spent even a few minutes on a visit.
My children were gone with families of their own so I moved her in with me.
We would have endless talks and take daily walks.

She didn't always recognize me, this was a sign that we didn't have much time left.
I promised myself that I wouldn't live to regret when her mind wasn't always clear.

I would play her old game to make her laugh and fill her with endless cheer.
I would like to say her very last days were filled with laughter and joy.
I'd enter her room and lift the gloom by playing her favorite game, and we would laugh and laugh til our sides hurt again.

Who Is She

Who is she that looks at me with tears in her eyes, and says it's no surprise she knows exactly how I feel.

Whether happy or sad or very mad, and I can't believe she's real.

She's full of respect and ever so proud of who I've become and how I turned out.

Her smile so bright and always ready to offer a kind word of advice.

When she dresses up for an evening out, she always looks so regal.

Though her general look is far from tacky, she's just short of being legal.

Her words of wisdom are old cliches, some that I don't understand.

She utters them softly and believes that at the appropriate time, I'll use her advice when I can.

She's the face in the mirror; the one in my mind, she's steady, honest and true.

My pal and my mentor, my friend and guide, always saying "I love you."

Though she's been gone a while I know for sure I'll see her on the other side.

And I'll thank her again as she greets me, and once again my Mother is my guide.

Grandma's Letter

My Grandmother was a wise old woman, I should have listened a little better.
She'd been gone a year when to my surprise I actually got a letter.
My hands were shaking as I broke the seal, looking at her beautiful script.
The tears started flowing as I read each word and tried to get a grip; on the pounding of my heart as I pictured her there.
She had a lot of rules for us to follow, and I tried so hard to be good.
She said to err is human and to forgive divine, but always remember to walk a straight line.
The road can get weary and very long, keep your heart open and burst into song. For the music of life is all about love.
She spoke of friendship and kindness, truth and love, and knowing God is watching from above.
It doesn't matter when you're gone how much wealth you had, the size of your house or your fancy car.
The only thing that matters is who you are. Were you fair with your family? Did you do what you need to help others in their journey to always succeed in reaching their goal? For this I believe is why we are here.
It's a bitter world we live in, we need more softness and open hearts.
Belief in yourself is where it starts.
Give til it hurts, smile through the pain, tell everyone they can turn things around.
Remember it's too late once you're under the ground.

Fifty Years

Too many times at weddings the witnesses make a toast, but often it seems like they're doing a roast. So I'd like to add a few special thoughts; about kindness, friendship, and love. Since we've been married for many a year and have seen it all.

From walking the floor with a baby who ails, to helping me now as I become frail.

Fifty years later I still can't forget, how you stole my heart on the day that we met. You were long and lanky with a huge boyish smile, as you stood there and watched me for such a long while.

We vowed our love to the very end, and to also remain the best of friends.

We've each done our share to further our love through the eyes of the children we bore, they make us proud of how they turned out, knowing it's what we wished for.

As a wife a mother, a teacher and nurse, I tried to handle with some class. My style is my own; I'm one of a kind so to this I'LL raise my glass.

And cheers to you my guy, raise your glass high. As a husband and father you're a teacher too, our children have learned from the best.

Now they are out in the world with families of their own saying "When did they get any rest?"

Fifty years went by so very fast look ahead to enjoy our future; we already have a fabulous past.

You're Gone

My dreams are shattered, my world has come apart as you left me today and broke my heart.
You're gone from me, no longer share our bed; but you're still right there inside my head.

I hear your voice, I can see your face.
Where are you now, and in what place?

Our life was good, we did so much.
Always with a loving touch.

You're gone from me and I miss you so.
I never believed you would really go.

Be at peace my love for we'll meet again.
I don't know how or when.

It's the circle of life, of love and such.
How I desperately crave your tender touch.
You helped me live a glorious life, shared my joy and sorrow.

But I alone face tomorrow.
The days will be long, and the ache will always be there, but I will carry on.

I'll talk to you daily and try not to cry.
Until me meet again, I'll have my memories to get me by.

My Eulogy

Have I ever told you how I really feel; I wish I had more life to live? But HE'S given me as much time as he can, so I'll tell you what's important to me so you'll always understand.

The amazing person has gotten me to where I can say; that after all these years one look at you still takes my breath away.

Be happy and smile after I'm gone and keep up with your favorite things. Play volleyball, pickle-ball, mess with the kids, and please try real hard not to sing.

Remember me telling you get out and find something to do, so make yourself smile it's just for awhile, until I'll be back with you.

Don't let the kids stop you or slow you down, if you find someone new in your life. They'll think it over and realize you've always been true to this wife.

You deserve the company of someone your age to walk and talk and be with so you never get real cranky. This doesn't mean cozy enough to encourage hanky-panky.

The important part is to be happy, as you've been all these years, it doesn't start and end with me, you'll see.

Music to my Ears

Sweet Adeline's are women who sing music like no other. They are girls from all walks of life.

Some are students and teachers, lawyers and preachers and more often a mother and wife.

Every Wednesday they meet, all 90 on their feet and what a glorious sound is heard.

The competition is high for these are the best, they have teachers and trainers who don't give them a rest.

They practice for hours to get the perfect sound, it's not always easy, but it will be found.

First it's learning your part of four-part harmony; this is not an easy thing. Then blending them all the director will call "Do it again" until they make it ring.

There are hours of work; costumes to wear, nails must be done, and oh yes the hair.

On stage it's a sight they all look alike, but what a show they will do. It seems they just started and so quickly they're through.

When you hear of Sweet Adeline's, or the BGC, make sure you get to go,
to hear the sound so sweet and pure, your heart will start to grow.

The BGC

The BGC is music to me that fills my soul and heart.

The blend of the voices so pure and true, a symphony from the start.

Listening to their music, like I do everyday, puts a smile on my face and my stress goes away.

So many girls from all walks of life, to do this without any pay.

They believe without doubt, that to sing, makes you happy all day.

I could live forever, happy to always be.

Listening to the sound of the BGC.

The 21st Century

To say the words we need to hear, without any prejudice or fear.
How can I be happy, instead I feel so sad.
The world is full of hatred, and everyone is mad.
We live in fear that each day will find terror of another kind.
Starvation in a world with plenty of food, homeless people with no place to go.
The sun's growing older, and the moon has lost it's glow.
Where is the peace that I crave so.

Politicians will rant on and build up walls, keeping out what they say doesn't belong.
But the countries and governments rulings of this have never been more wrong.
Start with the environment, clean up the waters and air.

Then we can breathe safely, and go from there.
Feed all the people and make them all well.
That would be a story to tell; our children's children and more years of peace,
prosperity and hope for all.
That man can live as I still recall.
NATO for nations and UNICEF for kids, these were great programs long ago.
Can we bring them back, start over again?

I can't believe it's too late.
If something isn't done relatively soon our demise will be our fate.

Lost Pride

I used to be proud of who I am to live in the USA. Now someone asks me where I'm from, and I'm very reluctant to say. We were the young country with high ideals, the dreams of a better life. Where it was fair and equal for all, without a whole lot of strife.

But the older we got the worse we became, until just like children we had no one to blame. We did it to ourselves, being arrogant and proud. Thinking we were better than others, but this isn't allowed.

In a world spent proving each is stronger than the rest, the wars we've gone through can only attest, to what can happen if you lose the respect of friendship worldwide, this we'll regret.

Our peace keepers have left, they've gone out the door, we now have antagonists filling the store. With bigotry and hatred, and rudeness to man, this was never part of the American plan. Let's bring back the kindness, stop bellowing loud. Apologize to countries we turned our backs on; they've been around the block a few times. Let's learn from their erroneous ways. If we clean up our act it could possibly be, we may live a few more days.

No more bluster and bragging about how good we are. All the years spent working to have countries get along; I don't know how it happened but it has all gone wrong. Now we're split again in a way that's not very healthy, and doesn't leave me feeling secure. But if we work fast and hard; to be safe, happy and free, of this I'm very sure.

America can be great again; we just need a new plan. Let's start from scratch, take smaller steps, and grow up to be a good man.

Going to War

How sad it is that once again we may go to war; and lose the men and boys we've gained, as we've done many times before. Every twenty years or so the men would start to gather, they would be shipped out as fast as possible to help their brothers when they would rather be staying home with wife and child keeping the home fires burning and making strides for peace on earth for which we all are yearning.

Politicians say it's the way of life, as parents shake with fear, that the son they raised so lovingly will one day disappear. To be lost in a land so far from home, and in fear of what's ahead. This is the nightmare that parents feel each night as they lie in bed. What do politicians know. their children won't be going, or if they do it won't be on front lines so you'll be knowing. They'll work in an office back in the states or a job that keeps them growing.

Your son and mine will be out on the line, from sunup to sundown waiting for things to get better. Then one day it comes and not your son, instead you get a letter.
Thank you for the service he's given, he's now a hometown hero. But, without one hand and missing two legs his chance for a full life is zero.

So think again you people in power of how you've shown our men, that honor and love of your country is your duty to defend.
This is your job to stop the insanity, It's you who need to mend the terrible turmoil the world is in.

So say a prayer for peace and show love to your brother, and cease the fear of every Father and Mother. This is when we win.

Troubled Thoughts

Some days I find it's hard to write my poetry and have it rhyme.
When I think of a subject to speak of, and not just to waste my time.
I've written about mothers and children; morals, respect and love, growing up, growing old, friendship and more.
Some poems were stories and others just a thought, so I put it on paper and that's when I read the thoughts that I couldn't get out of my head.
Of the old man who is lost, or the daughter who is missing, and of all the people in need.
I read the paper and wish I could help the family whose house burned and left them without shelter and food. With little children this is not good. They have no place to go, no money to spend on a room or hotel, when does it end.
There are animals abandoned by someone so mean, they weren't fed or sheltered, and never kept clean.
If we don't start to show that we really do care, how will our youngsters learn anywhere that this is our job, our responsibility.
One's lifetime is short to do all that needs to be done. To shape up the world and still have fun. But it can be done.
If every day we do one good deed, like donate a coat or a dinner to someone in need. Or maybe just listen to someone's pleas of a better way for you and me.
The quality of life isn't what you you have. It's what you put into it.
So put yourself out there, give til it hurts, overextend yourself.
In no time at all you'll feel an immense sense of satisfaction, that what started as just a tiny idea has become your main attraction.

What I Need

I wish there was peace in the world as our flag unfurled so all countries could be as one.

With hope for a future brighter than the past, that the wars will end the worst is over and at last we have become.

A universe of happiness, prosperity, and love for all. It's time we get along, with sisters and brothers of all ages and types, and the weak are carried by the strong.

When no one is better or less than another, equality for all is your dream. To be kind, show respect, and love to every person is not as difficult as it seems.

Leave it to those in charge is what we do hoping they'll do it right, but here I am writing and thinking always that our world is ready to fight.

To be first, to be best to, be stronger then the rest isn't what it seems if we end in oblivion because of bad judgment. This is my worst dream.

So be gentle and kind, say thank you,and please, three words that do so much.
Say them over and over and over again, you can ."I'm well, thank you."

Say "How are you" to even a stranger on the street. You'll be surprised how far kind words can go if you let them take the lead, and then maybe someday soon the headlines will read.

THERE'S PEACE ON EARTH GOODWILL FOR ALL!

This is what I need.

Ecology

I try to follow all the rules, I really don't see how.

I missed a few, who'd ever know there are so many now.

Recycle your papers and such but be sure they are clean.

No food remains stuck, no coffee grounds.

To me this simply seems easier to use plates and cups to be washed
but the young people are quite lazy.

Wash them they say, are you crazy?

A plastic bag wraps my paper each day that the young man hangs on my door.
So I save all his bags and hang them back out, so he can use them once more.

Plastic is buried that's no longer used, but oh we've done it this time.
They won't decompose if they're buried and cannot even be burned,
as this would effect out atmosphere most, the scientists already learned.

We've ruined that too, how evil is man to wreck this place we call home,
and it matters not where you live or where ever you may roam.

In no time at all our world could be gone, we are rushing to an end,
and whether rich or poor we all need to help to make our environment
our friend.

So pick up your trash, recycle your goods, tell others to do the same.

Start a "CLEAN UP YOUR WORLD" club, and don't be surprised to
hear people saying your name.

What could ever be better than this, but to leave the world a better place than
the one in which you exist.

Money

If we tax the rich like we did the poor, there wouldn't be any poor anymore.
Social Security is charged to the workers. They supported it all along. To not get back what is legally theirs is totally illegally wrong.

Politicians found a way to loophole our Social Security system, now the money is gone and they don't know how it got away. They'll just keep making more every day. They keep printing dollars like there's no tomorrow and giving their kids a free ride.

This is when I shouted "That's not what we need, it's just a budget on speed".
Let's take it slower, stop shouting and yelling, tell everyone to be patient and calm. We will do it as our forefathers taught us; with patience, virtue and honor. Our coffers will grow as the people learn; you can't spend it all or you'll have nothing in return.

Let's say we start everyone out at birth with two hundred fifty dollars and see what their parents do with it.
Will they bank it or invest it, how will they make it grow?
Will they spend it on frivolous things or something of importance?
I guess we will never know.
It would be nice if they could make it to the bank to deposit it and start an account to grow, forever gaining speed and something for their child to use in their time of need.
We gain more knowledge the older we get, but we need to teach all young people that money can't buy happiness.
If we show kindness and love for all the reward felt inside is humility and pride.
There is no better feeling, after all.

The Sewing Machine

I was maybe seven years old when I was taught to sew with only a needle and thread. Mother said learn it right for Grandma would see it and this was something I dread. She was very particular about the old ways, saying no one could do it like her.
Though I tried my best, I would fail every test when I pretended she was the judge, for the look I would see when she glanced at me, I knew she would never budge on her opinion of me and what I had done.

I made blouses skirts and dresses for all my dolls to wear, and matching headbands of the same cloth in which I'd tie their hair. My stitches were large and not very even, they had a way of going quite wild. So the clothes that they wore were a real eyesore, but not in the eyes of a child.

The hems were all crooked, there were holes in the sides, the stitches showed everywhere. But I was so proud of the job I had done,and to be honest I just didn't care. Until she was there!

It happened one day as I started to play. Grandma stopped in for a short little visit. She looked at my dolls all lined up on the couch, and said "Who made this and what is it?" She asked Mom where I was; and what I was doing, and said she wanted to talk just to me. So she took my hand and we walked outside to a tea party beneath a tree.

Grandma said that of all her fourteen grand kids no one ever sewed a thing, she said she would teach me all that she knew and I would inherit her sewing machine.

I still sew today on the same machine she left me years ago; and I think of Grandma each time the motor hums and the stitches start to flow.

Friend

Definition: a person attached by feelings of affections or personal regard.
A person who knows everything about you and loves you anyway.

A woman can do most anything; walk for miles, laugh, dance and sing. But without friends she won't have anything.

We go through life with the belief we've done our best. Yet in the end we'll fail the test, when asked what did you do to help others through to a life of joyful bliss? I'd quickly respond with a hug and a kiss. It's never enough.

To listen and learn what they're going through, and help to change things, is what a true friend would do. I was so sure I helped, but had not heard her words and got to my knees to pray. God said I got off the boat before it hit the shore, I'll tell you how to do more. Be a friend with compassion, respect, caring and giving to be the life I you want to be living.

I tried it His way and I can now say you listened with your heart and heard me true, and a friend forever I found in you.

My Friend

We met when we were only five. Kindergarten pals for life. I looked at her and it seemed to me she was most like the person I wanted to be. So dainty and pretty with manners above all, perfect in every way. She was better than a sister she was my best friend.

When I was hurting and thought no one could tell what I was going through. But she knew.

She would look at me with tears in her eyes and it was no surprise. She felt my pain and I would share her grief. It was always such a great relief.

She'd give me her smile always bright and ready and with encouraging words tells me so. Not mincing words saying get back on your feet, just give it a go.

We've gone through grammar and high school, marriage and children, good times and bad as well. She knows my insides are soft and always protected, with a hard exterior shell.

But my worst of times she's helped me back and I'll never be able to tell, of how she's helped me live to be my best, she's saved me at times from despair. Now it's time to say how much I care.

Which is something she knows, for she knows me so well.

Time goes by we're out of touch so I pick up the phone and call. She's right there waiting as I knew she'd be, says it's been too long after all. I know you so well and I could tell we need to get together.

She's my go to girl, my rock in a storm, her advice is always smart. Now I'll tell her how much I love her, and how happy she makes my heart.

Though she knows me so well, this time I'll tell.

My Friend Kim

She was sleeping when I got to my friend's room today.

I took one look and I began to pray.

She'd lost weight and I could immediately tell that her medicine wasn't working well.

They were making her comfortable so whatever it was made her keep nodding to sleep.

Her husband and daughters were at her side giving aid and showing their love.

They are two young ladies and it's hard to imagine how long it will take to heal, the heart that is broken because of the loss, and all the emotions you feel.

Her husband, a quiet man, only spoke three words as I offered my help and love.

He said, "It's too soon." I knew what he meant as he looked to the heavens above.

But my friend has been on a heavy road and given it the best she had.

She wouldn't condone our tears, they would actually make her mad.

The camping and phone calls and visits we've shared made us forget our sorrows.

And yet, here we are and it's sad to me, for there won't be any tomorrows.

The memories we made throughout the years will help us to smile again.

And I know I'll see her on the other side and I'll say "Hello my friend."

Cloudy Mind

My baby is lost, she's wandering around in her mind, how can I help her, and what can I find? To break the spell this has on her, it pains me so, you see. That if this was a child of yours, you'd feel just like me.

I could rant and rave and curse a lot, break things and scream and yell, but this won't help her mind be calm, so I'll sit with her and tell; of the good times and special moments that made her heart so glad, like the day she had her little girl was the best she'd ever had.

How do I teach her to say what she thinks, though it's not what others want to hear. If you don't say what you're feeling it will never be crystal clear. No one can hurt you, belittle and deride you, and think of you any less. So let them have it, give it your all, you'll find you will be blessed. With a mind that clears for having said what's locked so tight inside your head.

Try it a little, it will grow into a ball of fire, so if someone presumes you're an easy mark, they will feel your ire.

Don't back down; be true to you, for you're the only one that mattered. And I'll still be with you when it comes around, that the fog is finally shattered.

Feeling Blue

I haven't written words today, feeling kind of blue, thought It's better to reach out and ask "How are you?"

"Are you feeling well? Would you like to walk and quietly talk or maybe just sit a spell?"

When I am down and see a frown on someone's face, It lets me know I need to help and get them back in their right place.

Depression is a state of mind; we are all born with to some degree.

Some have more than others, and I'm grateful I can see.

That mine is minor, so if I can help, feel free to call on me.

We'll take a walk and have a talk; that's what friends are for; my heart is always open, just tap lightly on my door.

You'll get a hug, a warm welcome too, and then a smile to say, I'll be here when you need me without a moments delay.

I'll listen to your worries, these things that trouble you so, and hope by talking about it, some stress you can let go.

When we're done you will feel better, and I will be grateful too, that as a friend you asked for help, and I was able to.

I Love You Still

You've gone from me and yet I still yell "Come back." But you never will.
You moved far away, seems like yesterday, but the years have flown on by.

With a heavy heart I think on back and can't remember why.
You left so quickly, always on the run.
You said "Life's too short, I need more fun".

I gave you my love, yet you threw it away.
We argued and fought everyday.
But I love you still, and always will.

The days turn to months the months into years.
My anxiety grows along with my fears.
That you'll never return to this place I adore.
Where I'd promised to love you forever more.

If tomorrow comes and you arrive, on the doorstep of my life.
I'll be happy again to say welcome home and once more be your wife.
Because I love you still and always will.

Deep Thoughts

I can't always put into words what my heart would like to say, but sometimes a poem will say for me the thoughts that won't go away.

There are those who speak without a thought, never caring who they've hurt. There are others who'll never say anything wrong; but will all of a sudden blurt the unthinkable things you'd never expect. Leaving you stunned as you detect; they don't know how to say it and still show respect.

To speak one's mind without anger is truly a wonderful gift, to debate is great, but seldom is done. It's the moment of anger that is finally won, by the person so quiet it stuns everyone, when they open up and speak their mind. But it's unkind, for they know not how to do it.

A bad word in return will just start a fight, or a huge argument at best, then it takes so long to apologize that at times we seem to forget.

It can't be that hard to be nice all the time, it's being patient and gentle and kind. It's forgivable love, like we receive from above, that we all try so hard to define.

I feel like I'm always preaching and talking about kindness and such, and trying hard to convince others, I can never do it enough.

The golden rule is to treat others as you wish to be treated, and as my journey through life continues on, I promise to be the best I can be, and go right on singing my song.

Rotten Thoughts

So many rotten thoughts are going through my head.
Things I wish I hadn't uttered and others I should have said.
Like the time I hollered leave me alone, and you did, so I got mad. How would you know?
Your love is so deeply pure and true, how can I hope to explain to you.
I feel stifled and cornered like I was a child.
I don't want my words to be vicious or wild.
But know that I need my time alone, to center myself to be clear in my mind.
Then I will talk to you so gently and kind you'll think I'm so different from before. I'll put that other girl out and hope she won't show up anymore.
This state that I'm in leaves me mad all the time since I'm older and can't do much for myself.
You assure me it's okay, you like to help, as you wait on me like my personal elf.
I worry about you now, what happens to you when I'm gone?
I wish you days of joy and sunshine; I wish you peace of mind. You've done so much to enrich my life, you truly are one of a kind.
It was something you didn't do well but go ahead and sing and dance, you might even find romance.
The kids can't stop you from doing what you want they've already been told by me.
Cause when we all meet up in heaven I'll be the one you see.
Tell your stories and help everyone out, that's what you are all about. And as your days close down I'll wait for you and the gates will open and I'll walk you through.

Unfinished Arguments

I'm writing today to finally say the things that make me irate. There are so many that I'll start with me, and end with a whole lot of hate. But worry not, you aren't one of those things, but I think this will be great to just get it out of my head.

I hate people who sneer at things that they hear, but never say anything back, yet when they are asked, they put on a mask and change the subject and just yakity-yak. They go on about anything to never return to the topic already spoken. Seems they know a lot but won't share their knowledge, makes me think their brain is broken. There are others who love to disagree. They walk away, how do you think that leaves me?

Let's discuss our differences instead of bottling them up inside, where they fester and grow. They then become huge in strength and size, and the verbiage will never flow.

So again we're at an impasse where it's either ignored or starts; an argument of great proportions, and no love felt from the heart. How is it possible to forgive and forget, as the good book tells us to, when I ask what's wrong and you won't say what's truly bothering you?

Open up and spill it out, there's no reason to scream or shout. Let's talk like two adults, this is what friendship is all about.

My MRI

The thought of an MRI is a foreboding thing, creating a lot of fear.

Not only for the person involved but for everyone who holds you dear.

As I told my Mom of what I faced, I didn't want to know what was going through her head, that her face already showed.

She was scared for me so I could see I had to allay her fears, I told her it was precautionary and I would appreciate no tears.

We arrived on time at the appointment, to get the results I desperately need. To make me well and extend my life as the doctors all proceed, to look at the outcome of the MRI, I wish I knew how to read.

When I was a baby the surgeon said this will fix her heart, how would I know that forty years later, I was just off to a good start. So they fixed me well and without a fear I did all I wanted to do, I grew up and married and had my boys, but my world is now in doubt.

I trust God and my doctors to fix me again, but my inside voice wants to shout.

Dear Lord, help me heal, make me whole once again; my family counts on me every day. So please make me right with no bumps in sight, and try not to take me away.

I look again at my Mom and know how she must feel, as I would if I was in her place, but I see the love and her strength from above and I know whatever I face; she'll be there, and she'll care.

With my family all around we'll make it through, this is only a little glitch. Like the time I walked all the way home after putting my car in the ditch.

Just A Phone Call

I'm not asking for much just a phone call will do, just to stay in touch for I think about you.
When you're on my mind and we can't talk it's not like I can take a walk, and meet with you since you're far away, but on my mind most everyday.

Are you happy? Are you well, oh child of mine?

You left us here many years ago, to find your way in life, I hoped by now you'd find someone and bring her home as your wife.

Now I wait by the phone but it doesn't ring, you haven't called in awhile, but last time it was on the Internet, and I got to see your smile.

I hope you know I love you so, words alone can't say, how without you here my skies are gray.

I don't want you back if you don't want to be, just know how much you mean to me.

And how hard it is to set you free.

Moving Along

My mode of transportation has changed throughout the years, I've aged a lot but learning to drive, it was never something to fear.

As a young child I'd ride my trike, which then turned into a ten-speed bike. Public transportation was never a problem, we had streetcars than buses, taxis and more, or we'd use our feet to get to the store.

I learned to drive as a young adult, and it was a moment of joy as I did my best, and passed the final driving test.

I'm much older now and haven't been driving for awhile. It's not that I don't want to. The oxygen tank that accompanies me takes up too much space, and the walker I bring fills the rest of the car,so I'm out of breath and don't get far. Still there are family and friends who'll give me a ride when I have plans to go anywhere.

Today I received a scooter, now I'm running all over the place. If you see me out there you'll know I'm happy, they'll be a huge smile on my face.

It's been a quite a lesson, learning how to control it. I back it up and hit the wall, I pull forward and do the same, but it's not my fault there's so much power, the scooter is what I blame.

The controls take me from turtle to rabbit, and I can't seem to get a grip on the correct speed to always go, whenever I take a trip.

There is no manual so I don't have a way of knowing how fast I go. My husband says top speed is ten miles per hour, which I feel is way too slow.

My patient husband rides his bike and I take my little scooter, or he walks our dogs and I go along, something I couldn't do before.

So I back it up and hit the wall, pull forward to go out the door, but I miss again and try once more.

As I again hit the wall I'm really appalled, this is the third time today.

But we're now out the door as I loudly announce, hurry up and get out of my way!

Lunch With The Girls

My daughter picked me up for lunch today with a group of wonderful girls, I don't know from where they all came. But they were all dressed well, and greeted me nicely, and I can't recall even one name.

There were sixteen of them we met at eleven, at a restaurant in town. I knew this was trouble right from the start before I even sat down.

She teaches a class in exercise for women of a serious age. I can't be bothered; it's not my style, but they think she's quite the rage.

She's young and peppy so full of life, with two boys of her and a devoted wife.

But teaching old ladies to stoop bend and squat is not my idea of fun. Give me a bingo hall, or casino, to spend my money, or a beach just to stroll on, when the weather is sunny.

These women however enjoyed the lunch. They talked non-stop, what a crazy bunch! It was chaotic and noisy and lots of fun.

The poor waitress didn't know what to say when someone asked how will we pay? Write us separate checks please, it's easier that way.

When we got home my daughter asked if I had fun, I answered "Yes but really Hon, please don't ask me again til I'm at least one hundred and one."

Second Lunch With the Girls

She did it again as a nice surprise, I was given a ticket for lunch.
It would be special for Christmas and once again I'll be lunching with the whole bunch.
You remember the girls who talked and laughed so much.
I said I'd never go back yet here I was at their mercy.
Well the lunch started out just like the last, so much loud talking and yelling.
Their stories of Dawn and her exercise class all eighteen bursting with telling.
How funny are these athletes that stretch to a beat and call it exercising.
The YMCA is where they meet once a week to try to stay in shape by stretching and working their muscles.
They huff and they puff and work so hard to be better than before, when a nice long walk or a bicycle ride would accomplish so much more.
So we talk about the routine and how much they care, that Dawn is always waiting there.
One lady went to the washroom, she was gone for quite a while.
We were headed to find her when she walked in with a smile.
She said she was in the basement, that's where the elevator goes.
Why she wanted to see it, no one really knows.
They all ate their lunch including dessert, which I think is a riot.
For tomorrow they'll all be back in class to accommodate their diet.
Last time I told her I wouldn't be back, but these ladies are too much fun.
I'm not doing the class but I'll be back for lunch, I just can't resist this incredible bunch.

Third Lunch Date With the Girls

Once again I was going to lunch with the old lady exercise bunch.
This was okay ,it was a very hot day and was at a particular place.
My daughter drove to the house we were invited to, but was surprised by the look on my face.
I take my oxygen with me and use a walker, so how was I going to get from the car to the house over grass and stairs? This was starting to make me sweat.
Okay, so we made the walk with help from all which makes me feel quite needy.
As they set out the lunch my daughter says "Mother don't get too greedy".
Mind you, I eat like a bird, what was she thinking as I fixed myself a small plate.
I have never been told not to take too much, as I swore it would be my last date.
I proceeded to eat when a bee stung my knee and I spilled everything I had chosen.
By this time my oxygen had run out and I started to shout, hurry up get me something that's frozen.
I needed relief from the pain as I tried to regain a calm and normal feeling, and to replace my oxygen battery.
It was then I found the second one was already out of charge.
As I hustled to the car to plug myself in with the adapter I had brought, I said some things I shouldn't have and my cursing wasn't the best thought.
The ladies were appalled at my tirade but smiled and said not to fret.
They've all had days like these, ones they would like to forget.
Three women called when I got home to tell me it was quite entertaining, and thanks for the new curse words.They had forgotten a lot of them.
They are much older than me so I'll wait and see if they'll forget they met me.
And after a while, I'll say with a smile, I'm again having lunch with that crazy bunch.

Christmas Decor

I've checked all the boxes, I've hunted through all, to find my Christmas decor.
I've looked everywhere and was not surprised that I didn't have them anymore.
Could this be something I'd never need once we moved to the "Home"?
Again it's something he gave away, or threw out like before.
My bushy greens with lights attached; that I yearly hung everywhere, and the three boxes of picks to add glitter and glow with such a decorative flair.
Now I have to decorate our apartment door, there's a prize for the best one done.
He's made three trips to the store to replace my stock, and I haven't even begun.
The first greens he bought were skimpy and thin, even he knew they weren't acceptable. But he smiled and said "I'll be right back" as he ran back out the door.
I hustled to get done as much as I could before he came back with more.
I knew it would take me at least a week to decide what I wanted to do, but his idea was "Let's get it done, I'm going to be here to help you."
"Oh boy" I said, "that would be great" as I slapped myself in my mind.
I couldn't say I'd rather do it alone, that would have been unkind.
So I watched him work as he sprayed on the snow, and tried to help with the glue gun.
The problem was he wore more glue than the greens and the blisters he wore were no fun.
Back to the store for lights and batteries, this was his third major run; but it was while he was gone I accomplished a lot and had it already done.
We're told it's very pretty, festive and gay.
It might even win a prize on the judging day.
But that's not important to me really.
The thing is we did it together, I couldn't have done it myself.
So I thanked him and said how happy I was to have my own Christmas elf.

It's Almost Christmas

Three days from now and I'm not ready yet for the Holiday cheer and gifts I will get. As I wrap all my gifts to give to the children visions from years ago come to my mind. The memories are tender their joy so complete when they look at the tree and see at their feet all the gifts lying there.

They were told Santa would bring only a few since he had so many kids to deliver to. But oh how could they rest, thinking this Christmas could count as being the best. All seven came down to sit on the stairs and wait for us to rise. They opened their stockings hung round the door, surprised for what was inside.
Dad would rush in and light up the tree, and say "Okay send them in to me."
The looks on their faces took my breath away to see all the gifts Santa left that day.

We'd have a special breakfast and get ready to go, off to church to express with love,,our thanks for the reason we had our yearly Christmas season.
Then off to both Grandparents to share with delight the love of our families, this continued all night. Finally heading back home it was abundantly clear this is my favorite time of the year. Everyone's happy and it's not about gifts, it's the strong feeling of peace and love.

The children were dragging but went in to see everything was still there under the tree. We were all exhausted but ever so glad for the very special Christmas we just had.
Getting into pajamas and bowing his head, "Happy Birthday Jesus," the youngest one said at the end of his prayer as he crawled into bed.

Christmas, All is Forgiven

It was bedtime at last and to my delight, they all went to bed without a fight.
Of course they thought they'd been good and would harvest a heap, of gifts in the morn, left there while they sleep.
I tell myself it's the right thing to do, spending way too much money on the toys that they knew, would keep them busy for an hour or two.
Christmas is always the biggest day in our home, since a Birthday is the other day for presents. Going all year they wait with the greatest of hope believing Santa is some kind of dope, to think they were were good a whole year.
But it's Christmas so all is forgiven.
We went to midnight mass so the children could have their morning free, to spend with the gifts they found under the tree.
They couldn't sit still, kept fussing in church, I'm appalled at the looks we were given.
I said to myself to take it in stride, it's Christmas so all is forgiven.
Then it's off to two different grandparents houses, for a visit and a six-course dinner.
We head to the second house and even more food, now I know I'll never be any thinner!
By the time we get home the kids are asleep and need to be carried to bed, and the last thing I thought as I put them all down and couldn't get out of my head.
Is that it's Christmas so all is forgiven.

Christmas at Home

In 1968 we bought our first home and left it fifty years to the date. And I without a thought of what I'd give up, there wasn't even a debate.
When we moved in the first time with so little to start, and even less this time which broke my heart. All I can say is we did it anyway.

Now it's Christmas time and I think back when, the children were small and all of their belief in Santa Claus meant they would get something good. We didn't do a lot of presents, there was enough for three each, and they were thrilled with what they received. But inside I hurt for I believed it wasn't enough. We added two more to the group and now we're at seven. Going to church I prayed to heaven, you have an option Lord. Help me do this, I'm worn out, my pockets are empty. He asked, "What's it about?"
It's about giving, and I don't have a thing. "Look at your hands." And I saw my rings. That was a memory I will never forget, it is more important that I spoke to God than the rings I regret.
They would come down to wake us, and sit on the stairs all excited about what they had in their stockings which hung on the door frame. When they were done they'd wake us and say, "Good morning Mom and Dad, it's Christmas Day!" Dad would go in and light the tree, and in they would come excited to see, so many presents wrapped special for each.
He'd look at me with wonder, how could I have accomplished this? I wouldn't tell him, he'd feel so sad, and on Christmas Day that would be bad.
We visit the families and head back home with everyone following behind. The theme of the day would be nice to believe that everyone could be kind.
Our apartment is one of 125, these people have friends and families they see weekly and often daily. Yet on a holiday week, I'm always surprised not to see these people who love them.
This is the year of the COVID flu virus, and no one seems to care, that Christmas is here and I truly fear that the flu is what we share. All the people are staying home, no one is out and about. Our apartment has people waiting to see if any will come to see them, and I've already started hating. The hardest part of what I view is all the hours of waiting. To watch the clock and no one comes is more than I can stand. To this I want to add: if they can't be here at Christmas time they should be banned. From everything the apartment allows, that would treat them right. But the person waiting and watching the clock would still watch through the night.
If you have someone or know someone who's living alone today, please call them up, wish them a Merry Christmas and promise to come right away.

Hushed In The Dark

Everyone else was already in bed. But we whispered and conspired of things to be done when the new day dawned with the rising sun.

We were good children as a rule, but the day had came as we walked to school. We shared our plan with those who would listen and soon everyone agreed that the plan was good the time was right and we would pursue it after school. We all brought live chickens to school and put them in our locker. There were no holes in the locker so it couldn't get out, and this wasn't something we worried about.
We thought in the morning it would be fun to see all the girls and teachers run from the angry birds, who were pulled from their nest and given a horrid spot to rest. How could we not foresee the horrible outcome that it turned out to be.

We got there early so we could have our laugh. As we approached, we watched the Janitor move to the first set of lockers. The smell was the worst, that's when he cursed and said he'd find out who did it, and they would pay and rue the day they messed with Sammy Smittit. We were so scared, Mr.Smittit, was always angry and ready to blame the kids. Now he had a reason to find us out, and then we'd really hear him shout, of how he wanted justice.
He opened all the lockers and removed all the dead birds, cleaned up everything, but no one let on who did it.

Five years later we graduated from school ready to make our mark in life. All ten of us were ready to leave at the crack of dawn, to the big cities and further on. We had our breakfast and said our good-byes and getting into the car, noticed an odor. It burned our nose and our eyes and I already knew, it was Mr. Sshmitit and this was deja vu. Popping the trunk we found ten baby skunks, this was too much to expect. I laughed and said we so deserved it, and put it to the test. As each gave their word that it was now over and we've put it all to rest.

But I've been thinking a lot about Mr. Smittit and think it's only fair, that he should reap the benefit of something very rare. I'll be sending him a post with something to share . This will have me laughing so rich, I can finally say, "Payback is a bitch.."

Made in United States
North Haven, CT
13 November 2021